# Love

## The Blessings of Angels

### Angela Wells

Published by Mystic Mouse® Publishing in 2014
www.MysticMouse-Publishing.com

Text Copyright © 2014 Angela Wells

Image Copyright © 2014 Mystic Mouse® Design

*First Edition*

The author and publisher accept no responsibility for how you might use the images or information contained herein or any results that may occur.

It is the intention of the author to offer only general help & guidance towards your physical, mental, spiritual & emotional growth and wellbeing.

# Index of Messages

| | | |
|---|---|---|
| 1 Strength | 22 Responsibility | 43 Inspiration |
| 2 Balance | 23 Play | 44 Faith |
| 3 Communication | 24 Tenderness | 45 Gratitude |
| 4 Support | 25 Grace | 46 Efficiency |
| 5 Freedom | 26 Delight | 47 Wisdom |
| 6 Love | 27 Compassion | 48 Joy |
| 7 Understanding | 28 Enthusiasm | 49 Trust |
| 8 Abundance | 29 Illumination | 50 Light |
| 9 Humility | 30 Education | 51 Peace |
| 10 Purpose | 31 Willingness | 52 Clarity |
| 11 Transformation | 32 Flexibility | 53 Truth |
| 12 Music | 33 Self Worth | 54 Purification |
| 13 Adventure | 34 Meditation | 55 Honesty |
| 14 Release | 35 Blessings | 56 Bliss |
| 15 Devotion | 36 Commitment | 57 Acknowledge |
| 16 Miracles | 37 Courage | 58 Healing |
| 17 Charity | 38 Justice | 59 Simplicity |
| 18 Mercy | 39 Humour | 60 Happiness |
| 19 Power | 40 Harmony | 61 Prayer |
| 20 Hope | 41 Beauty | 62 Patience |
| 21 Creativity | 42 Comfort | 63 Acceptance |

## Foreward

*I met Angela when she attended one of my workshops in 2008. I love the energy that radiates from her and she is clearly a sensitive soul. She has true empathy for others and understands what they are going through. Angela always reaches out when she can; sharing her gifts, experience and knowledge.*

*Angela is a Healer and believes it is one of the greatest gifts to be a channel for healing which can bring such relief and peace. She also loves giving healing to animals and is a wonderful Medium and talented Angel Card Reader.*

*I know Angela loves bringing through poetry & other inspired writings, and it is the latter that you will find beautifully presented throughout this book. The inspired messages started to flow many years ago when Angela met an old lady called Miriam. They chatted after services at the local spiritual church and this led to regular discussions over tea and cake. They sat in meditation and it wasn't long before the Angels started to connect and Angela started to write the words and inspirations that flowed. The two friends had both suffered tragedies & heartbreak and they felt blessed & privileged that Angels would connect with them in this way bringing such words of comfort, enlightenment and wisdom.*

*Angela has waited a very long time for these words to be shared and I am so pleased for her, and you, that these lovely Angelic Blessings are now available in this unique, stunning and inspiring book. I also know that Angela's greatest wish is that the words, colours and imagery bring you guidance, healing & upliftment and help you in your daily life.*

*My hope is that you will receive the Love from them and enjoy them in any way you can so you too may receive their Blessings in Your Life...*

*Much Love & Many Blessings*
White Elk Woman

## Who is White Elk Woman?

White Elk Woman is the inspiration behind and co-creator of the Crystal Skull Message Cards & Meditation Book, the Crystal Skull *ShadowLight* Cards and a Personal & Planetary Healing CD. She is also a facilitator of transformational talks & workshops.

*"Bridging the worlds of Spirituality & Entrepreneurship; proving that spiritual people can create the life they desire."*

Visit her website where she has created a number of FREE videos and other bonuses especially for you!

Simply leave your name and email address at *www.TheEntrepreneurialLightworker.com*

## Special thanks to the following people for supporting this book…

### Miss Angel's Vintage Emporium
An eclectic mix of vintage and retro clothing, jewellery and accessories.
Website: www.vintagemave.co.uk

### Personal Paranormal
"Personal, because we care"
West Midlands based spiritually led paranormal group
Tel: 07419 - 129737 Email: info@personalparanormal.co.uk
Website: www.personalparanormal.co.uk

### Darran Charles
Caring, sensitive, Medium & Clairvoyant
Tel: 07554 - 173575
Facebook: www.facebook.com/medium.darran
Email: mediumdarran@gmail.com
Website: www.mediumdarran.tk

## Angela and her Angels

*Angels have always been a huge part of my life. Even as a child I was fascinated by them. I would often hear or read things about them or see pictures of them. I felt that they watched over us and looked after us as attendants of God.*

*My maternal grandmother was a huge part of my childhood and through books I read, along with things I learned from her, I grew up believing in the afterlife. I called it 'Happy Land'. It seemed quite natural to me that we would pass onto another place to carry on with our lives once this one was over. I thought "if God created us for this World he would not just let us die, that would be too final". It may have been this kind of thinking that made me feel quite alone at times and I did not fit in with other children at school, but, I loved spending time with my grandmother, chatting with her, and of course…with my Angels!*

*My grandmother moved to 'Happy Land' when I was seventeen and I missed her terribly, but I carried on with my life knowing that she was there watching over me and guiding me through life's lessons – of which there were many, both physically and emotionally. But, I never ever lost my Faith.*

*Eventually, in my mid-forties, I found out about spiritual churches and my spiritual journey began in earnest. I became a Healer and have spent a long time developing as a Medium. I love learning and discovering new things and find it funny that the more I learn the less I seem to know!*

*I still sit in Meditation and it is through this that the Angels came and brought these Blessings of Love and Wisdom for you. It's thanks to a lovely lady called Miriam, that you are reading this today, as it was her who sat with me and held the space for the words to flow.*

*Every day I say thank you for the Gift of a new day and for the experience and joy of learning. I feel humbled to be able to be of service; to give and share Love – the greatest lesson we learn while we are here, on Earth, walking our Spiritual and Universal Pathway.*

## Before working with this book

You may wish to hold the book to your heart when you first receive it and bond with it in a positive and loving way, holding the intention that the pages within will always work with you for the highest good of all concerned.

If you are going to be using the Angels when working with other people, either for healing, guidance or meditation then you might like to sit with one or two different Angel Blessings each day and really get to know the healing energy and information that each one brings through.

Every Angel has some thoughts for you to ponder, but you may well find that each time you work with them, even if the same one comes up for you, it may well be bringing you a different message. You may also find that you are drawn to the same line over and over and this may well continue to happen until you have truly understood or integrated that particular piece of wisdom. Just go with the flow and learn to trust that what is given is exactly as it should be.

Before choosing an Angel Blessing to work with, sit quietly, relax and take a few deep breaths. Ask to be connected to the Angelic Kingdom in order that they work with and through you in the best way possible at this time.

Hold a clear intention of what it is you would like to receive guidance or healing on during a session. Then, when you feel ready, just start to flick through the book and see where you 'land'. You may be drawn to the image in the top right hand corner or the coloured hearts at the edge of the page, or the book may just fall open at a particular place. You may even hear or see a number in your head.

There is no right or wrong way to use this book, just go with what you feel is right and true in your heart and let the Angels do the rest…

## Using this book

*The following pages provide some basic information to get you started, but the more you work with these Angel Blessings, the more you will understand their vibrations. Each image is accompanied by words of support, guidance, and, in particular, a message of Love from the Angels. The colour vibrations, as well as their accompanying words, can also be used to bring about healing on many levels.*

*Working with the imagery, you could...*

♥ *Focus on the colours and feel the energy wash over and through you*

♥ *Place the coloured page within your aura as you feel guided*

♥ *If working with a client, breathe in the colour(s) and blow the vibrations into their aura*

♥ *Pick a point on the page and stare at it, letting your focus soften and then allow your mind to wander as you go into a visual meditation*

## Messages of Love

Each Angel image comes with a Message of Love. You could try working with some of these and create an appropriate affirmation. For example :-

♥ LOVE is accepting one another – could become "I am Love and I accept others"

♥ LOVE can pursue a dream – could become "I am Love and I am pursuing my dream"

♥ LOVE is amazing – could become "I am Love and I am amazing"

Equally you can just as easily use the keywords such as Miracles, Abundance, Creativity, Tenderness etc. and create something very simple like :-

**"I embrace Miracles" - "I am Abundance"**
**- "I am Creativity" - "I am Tenderness"**

Or you might like to try using a number of the keywords together to create a longer affirmation. For example:-

**"I believe in Miracles as I embrace my Creativity**
**and manifest Abundance & Tenderness in my life"**

## Chakras and Colours

*This section provides some basic guidelines as to how the colour vibrations can relate to the chakras and consequently various parts of your body (as well as states of mind, spirit or emotion). By integrating the various colour vibrations, you can help to bring harmony to certain areas.*

*If you feel you are lacking in a particular aspect of your life, or a certain chakra needs a boost then the colour tabs on the edge of each page provide an example of some colours you may wish to consider working with. As always, there is no absolute right or wrong way to work with these, so just allow yourself to be a clear channel, trust, and let the Angels and colours speak to you.*

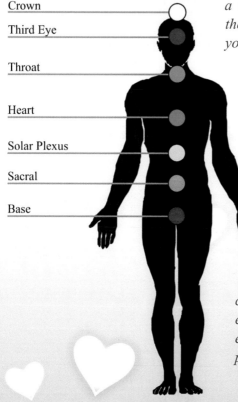

Crown

Third Eye

Throat

Heart

Solar Plexus

Sacral

Base

*A list of the seven main chakras along with their approximate positions is included in this section. You can also find examples of the things that might be experienced if a chakra is out of balance and how bringing appropriate colours into the related chakra can potentially enhance certain traits or emotions and aid certain physical issues.*

## 1. Base

**Some signs of imbalance may be:** *instability, insecurity, hunger or weight gain, lower back/leg/knee/spine problems, constipation, inability to manifest or move forward.*

**Energising Colours:** *Red, brown and earthy colours - can instil grounding, stability, stamina, motivation, purpose, strength, manifestation.*

## 2. Sacral

**Some signs of imbalance may be:** *jealousy, frustration, sexual problems and allergies. Skin, bladder and lower intestines may also be affected.*

**Energising Colours:** *Orange & autumnal colours - can instil joy, respect for oneself, creativity, cheer, pick-me-up, happiness. Can help to release stored negativity.*

## 3. Solar Plexus

**Some signs of imbalance may be:** *fear, lack of confidence, perfectionism, low self esteem, diabetes, ulcers. Digestion, nerves, liver and muscles can also be affected.*

**Energising Colours:** *Yellow and golden colours - can instil happiness, cheer, focus, will(power), enthusiasm, energy, self worth, mental clarity.*

## 4. Heart

**Some signs of imbalance may be:** *emotionally unstable, overly critical, inability to show or receive affection. Heart, arms, hands, blood and circulation can also be affected.*

*Energising Colours:* Green & pink - can instil love and trust in yourself & others. Harmony, peace, abundance, new beginnings. Can help to release heart related emotions.

## 5. Throat

*Some signs of imbalance may be:* communication issues, little discernment, ignorance. Thyroid, ear, neck, shoulder, lung, and throat can also be affected.

*Energising Colours:* Blue & turquoise - can instil a release of physical tension, better communication, peace, healing, honesty, calming, cleansing.

## 6. Third Eye (Brow)

*Some signs of imbalance may be:* cynicism, fear, lack of concentration, feeling detached, headaches, eye/nose problems (especially left eye), vivid or unpleasant dreams.

*Energising Colours:* Indigo & purple - can instil a sense of responsibility, spiritual transformation & understanding; also powerful vision, clairvoyance, wisdom.

## 7. Crown

*Some signs of imbalance may be:* depression, lack of enthusiasm/ inspiration, migraines, problems with right eye, forgetfulness, psychological imbalance, confusion.

*Energising Colours:* White or magenta & ultra violet - can instil clarity, cleansing and purity. Connection to Source / Divine guidance & universal energy.

## *The Aura*

*The body is not just physical, but is made up of various 'energetic' layers that can't usually be 'seen'. These layers make up the aura (also known as the auric field) and are called subtle energy bodies. Each layer relates to different aspects of the self. There are many subtle bodies, but most healers will perceive or work with the four main bodies (listed below).*

***1. The etheric body*** *sits within and directly around our physical body. This can be up to about an inch away and is the first part of the aura that people will sometimes actually see - often as a white, fuzzy glow around someone. It introduces energy to the physical and we can perceive the health and vitality of a person in this body.*

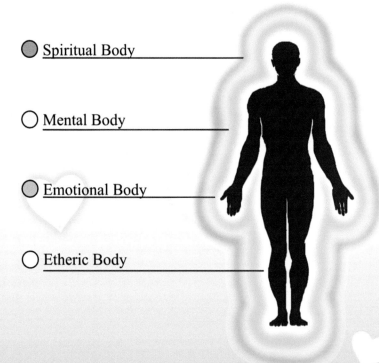

○ Spiritual Body _____

○ Mental Body _____

○ Emotional Body _____

○ Etheric Body _____

**2. The emotional body** *is where we hold most of our emotions, dreams and illusions. It is generally a few inches away from the physical. When linked in and giving healing, it can often be perceived either visually or simply as an intuitive sense of where it is.*

**3. The mental body** *is slightly further out again and can be perceived in the same way. It is where our conscious and sub-conscious thoughts are held, both past and present. A finer vibration than the emotional, it can be perceived as bright yellow if it is healthy.*

**4. The spiritual body** *generally holds most of the wisdom and knowledge. This layer helps us acknowledge and bring in our guidance, angels and higher self etc. It is perceived as very pale hues of colour.*

*The etheric body feeds vitality to the physical body, while the emotional body can help bring creativity. The mental body can assist with structured thinking and the spiritual body is associated with wisdom. The emotional and mental bodies are quite strongly linked and it is often within one of these bodies that dis-ease starts. The aura can get very 'clogged & dirty'. This can come about through encountering negative people, places or thoughts. Working with particular Angels and colours can help to clear and balance the energy bodies within the aura, thus leading to an overall sense of vitality and well-being on all levels.*

## *Meditating with the Angels*

*Sometimes just the act of meditating can seem to dissolve a problem. It can create a great space for dealing with issues in your life and accessing your deep well of inner resources. The Angels are always there with guidance if we just remember to ask!*

*Have you ever been in a situation where a friend has come to you with a problem and you can see the solution straight away? It seems so obvious that you wonder why they can't see it.*

*The issue is that they have become stuck IN the problem. When you are stuck IN a problem, all you can see is the problem. You can't see the solution because the solution is always 'outside' of the problem. The Angels always know the solution, as do you, but sometimes you can get so stuck in your problem you just can't figure out what to do.*

*So, put a thought out to the Angelic Kingdom and when you land on your page in this book just see what words you are drawn to. There maybe just one word or one line that jumps out, or three or four. If you wish you can then go deeper with these, perhaps go into meditation and ask the Angels to explain further the guidance they are trying to bring you or allow them to take you on a journey so you can understand the meaning at a higher level of awareness.*

## *Focus on a solution*

*Once you are able to step outside of a problem, you can start to tap into your inner resources to find the best solution.*

*You will find that some of the Blessings and messages in this book are fairly direct, whilst others are vague or ambiguous. This gives your mind & soul the opportunity to stretch out and get creative. Feel free to interpret the Angelic Blessings and inspired words in any way you like. Look to expand your possibilities. Illuminate new pathways, ideas and ways of dealing with things easily & effortlessly. And remember, the Angels are always with you...*

# Messages

## from the

# Angels

# Strength

LOVE only grows stronger

# *Strength*

Support is coming in all directions

Inner strength resists all fears

Strength brings you courage to face adversity

Be firm – stand your ground

Be fearless, time to go forward

Put your hand in the hand of God

Angels surround you as your shield

Endurance to achieve and accomplish what needs to be done

Do not give in or give up

## LOVE only grows stronger

LOVE is

*Balance*

to unburden

# ☙ 2 ❧
## *Balance*

Angels are weightless

Walk and talk within Nature

Create balance in all areas of your life

Letting go, letting God

Learn to forgive

Do not hold on to worries and burdens

Weigh up all sides

Release all to the power of the Universe

Travel lighter

LOVE is to unburden

# Communication

LOVE talks in all languages

# 3

## *Communication*

Walk your talk

Listen to sounds of the Universe

God communicates on all levels

Express yourself wisely and well

Speak from the heart

You can always ask for the right words to be given to you

Talk with your Angels daily-they will leave you signs

Words can be mightier than the sword

Contact another

LOVE talks in all languages

# Support

LOVE will assist you

# ❦ 4 ❧
## *Support*

You are never alone

Walk and talk with your Angels

God never deserts or forsakes you

Trust in Divine intelligence

Help may come from near or far

Give help to those you see in need

Comfort comes on Angels wings

God's hand is holding you steady

Look in all directions of the Universe

## LOVE will assist you

# Freedom

## LOVE has no agenda

# ❦ 5 ❦
# *Freedom*

Do not feel trapped

Value freedom

Do not take on board worries, burdens of others or the world

Allow yourself to be free

Do not give your power to anyone

God allows everyone to be free

Angels travel light

Allow your mind to soar like a bird

Your body, soul and mind will feel so much better

LOVE has no agenda

*Love*

LOVE is all

# 6
# *Love*

Universal language

Love heals all wounds and ills

Love is a key

Love is a healing balm

An energy of God

Love is all creativity

Love is unconditional

Angels created in images of love

Love is the answer

## LOVE is all

# *Understanding*

## LOVE is accepting one another

# 7

## Understanding

Understanding is acceptance of knowledge

Learning lessons

God's will

Know and understand yourself

Acceptance — how we perceive

Know the difference

It's better to understand than be understood

Angels understand who and where we are

Do not be judgemental or critical

LOVE is accepting one another

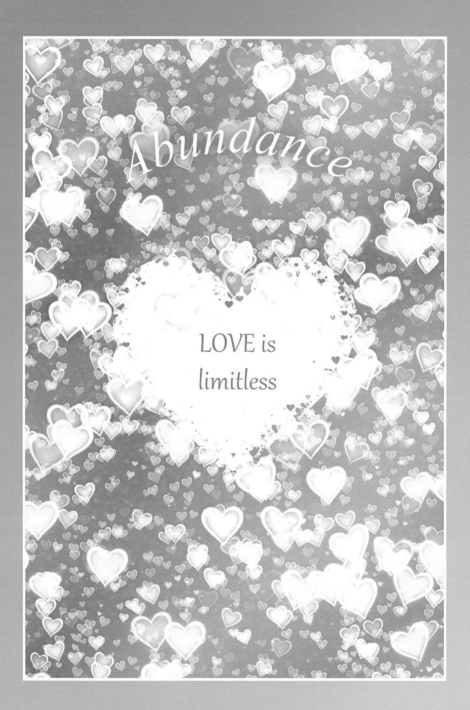

Abundance

LOVE is
limitless

## ❦ 8 ❧

# *Abundance*

Abundance awaits to be invited

Always give in abundance

With pure heart

Angels always bring in abundance

God loves a generous giver

However much you give, will always return

The richest gifts are those that money cannot buy

The Universe has many treasures

Value yourself for others to value you

LOVE is limitless

# *Humility*

LOVE has no need for ego

## ❧ 9 ❧
# *Humility*

Humility is pride without vanity

Serving others without intent of fame or fortune

Humbleness does not carry ego

Without humility we have no understanding

Humbleness shows beauty in the character

Accept your daily duties however great or small

God respects our humble nature

We are not higher or greater than Universal power

Angels know their place

LOVE has no need for ego

# Purpose

## LOVE can pursue a dream

# ❧ 10 ❧
## *Purpose*

Have an aim in life

Enjoy the journey along the pathway of life

Always be willing to learn

Confide in God if you get stuck

All Angels have a role

You can always change direction

The Universe has many answers

Stop, look and listen

Always strive with the best intention

LOVE can pursue a dream

# Transformation

LOVE changes everything

# ❦ 11 ❧
## *Transformation*

Transform your thoughts and feelings

Change begins within

Healing thoughts

Healing heart centre

Breathing exercises and techniques

God will help you to transform

Angels welcome change

Behold; butterfly release

Look, think and talk in love

## LOVE changes everything

Music

LOVE comes together at the right time

# ❦ 12 ❧
# *Music*

Listen to the natural sound of our world

Bringing joy, harmony and upliftment

God is always surrounded with melody

Angelic music always heard around the spheres

Music is an expression of how we think, see and feel

A creativity that touches heart, soul and mind

When feeling out of step, music will ease you back

into the rhythm of life

The maestro knows how to bring all the notes together

to perform a masterpiece

So pleasant to the ear which can still a busy mind

LOVE comes together at the right time

Adventure

LOVE is a world of opportunities

# ❧ 13 ❧
# *Adventure*

Life itself is an adventure

When stuck, take a look at the map of life

God will always be your guide

Adapt and be resourceful

Encourage imagination in a child

Angels are always prepared

Do not be afraid – seek support or ask for assistance

To gain experience, travel further afield

You never travel alone

## LOVE is a world of opportunities

# Release

### LOVE is to let go

# ❦ 14 ❧
## *Release*

Learn to forgive

Let go of fears and doubts

Allow God's love to envelop you

Open your heart and expand

Angels travel free

Free the past- move forward

Don't live in the past or borrow from the future

Be in the moment

Move forward with the flow

LOVE is to let go

# Devotion

LOVE is attentive

# ❦ 15 ❧
## *Devotion*

Dedicated to the task in hand

Adore the truth of God

Devote oneself to be of service to humanity

Angelic loyalty

God's devotion to this world is everywhere

A commitment with love

Being attentive and dutiful

Devotion is given to all those we love and care for

Serving with loyalty, obedience and trust

## LOVE is attentive

*Miracles*

LOVE is amazing

# ❧ 16 ❧
# *Miracles*

Miracles happen when you believe

Open your eyes – miracles are everywhere

Angelic magic

God performs miracles all the while

Miracles are not exclusive

Acknowledge miracles as gifts from Divine Source

Believe as children

Allow miracles to work for you

Be ready to receive a miracle

## LOVE is amazing

# Charity

## LOVE does not ration

# ❧ 17 ❧
# *Charity*

No strings attached

Be generous, good and kind

Offer help, assistance and support

Always be ready and willing to help all those less fortunate

God offers support day and night

Don't be too proud to ask if needed

Angels will not let you struggle

Gift aid

Charity may begin at home – be alert to another's call

## LOVE does not ration

# Mercy

LOVE is tender

# ❧ 18 ❧
## *Mercy*

Have and show consideration for others

God shows mercy with our vulnerability

Compassion and tenderness are qualities we need to nurture

Mercy is not a sign of weakness – it can be a strength

Mercy can be an attribute of one's character

Learn to be merciful at all times

Angels will teach us the way

In grief, mercy will sustain you

An indulgence of compassion and understanding

LOVE is tender

# Power

LOVE is Divine power

# ❧ 19 ☙
## *Power*

Power is a creative source

Use your power wisely and well

Power can bring light into darkness

May Angelic power uphold you

Power of God is infinite

Power encourages spiritual growth

Power is only lent

How powerful the word and hand of God

Power is an energy to embrace the Universe with light

## LOVE is Divine power

# Hope

LOVE is beyond our wildest dreams

# ❧ 20 ❧
# *Hope*

You can cling to hope when all is lost

Hope is God's encouragement to keep going

All is not in vain

There is light at the end of the tunnel

Bringing joy to a new day

Hope is the encouragement to walk another mile

In anticipation – relieving anxiety

Hope is an energy that helps build a dream

Angels hope to hear from us

LOVE is beyond our wildest dreams

# Creativity

LOVE is a work of art

# ❧ 21 ❧
## *Creativity*

Creativity is a gift to share with all

Creativity is an energy from the Divine Source

Don't hide your light under a bushel

Open your eyes as you look all around you

Creation is an expression of progress

Take time out to study

An inspiration from God

Work of Angels

An opportunity to discover your talents

LOVE is a work of art

# *Responsibility*

LOVE brings awareness

# ❦ 22 ❧
# *Responsibility*

God will leave us in charge when he trusts us

Look at every aspect

Angelic duty

If you are unsure, always seek higher intelligence

Responsibility should not weigh you down

Others rely upon you

Start each day in prayer and meditation

Make a commitment

Uphold any law or vow

## LOVE brings awareness

# Play

LOVE is magical

# ❦ 23 ❧
# *Play*

Set aside time to enjoy

Be in touch with your inner child

Relax, sing, dance, smell a flower

Playfulness is the lighter side of an Angel

God loves to hear your laughter

Playing allows your creativity to expand

Discover the world through the eyes of a child

Take time out – you will be more refreshed

Take a regular break – you will look at all with new eyes

LOVE is magical

# Tenderness

LOVE is to be gentle

# ❧ 24 ☙
# Tenderness

The need to be gentle

Gentleness within

Be gentle with one another

A need to be gentle with a baby or a child

Nurture a new-born baby, or idea

Birth of all nature – plants, trees and animals

Angelic touch

God's ways are always gentle

Tenderness is an emotion within the heart

## LOVE is to be gentle

# Grace

LOVE is exquisite

# ❦ 25 ❧
## *Grace*

Offer a prayer in thankfulness

Acknowledge the many numerous gifts at hand

God provides all your needs

Help always comes when most needed

Be more open and responsive

Look with Grace - you will always see beauty

Benevolence is kindness from the heart

Angels carry their gifts with Grace

In simplicity you will find Grace

## LOVE is exquisite

# *Delight*

## LOVE is enchanting

# ❧ 26 ☙
## *Delight*

Angels spread joy and happiness

Delight is pleasing to the ear and eye

God brings upliftment to your heart and mind

Listen to the sounds of Nature

Clear your mind and allow new to enter

Enjoy a favourite past time or pastime

Share a special moment

Give and receive with joy

Be really pleased and elated

## LOVE is enchanting

# Compassion

LOVE grows more tenderly

# ❦ 27 ❦
## *Compassion*

Compassion is understanding with empathy

Feel and offer sympathy

Love dearly and tenderly

Angelic healing

Within God's tender care

Love we feel for all those suffering

There is no love without compassion

Have compassion for those who dislike or persecute you

May compassion grow within your heart

LOVE grows more tenderly

*Enthusiasm*

LOVE is sensational

# ❦ 28 ❧
## *Enthusiasm*

Be eager to learn and progress

Be keen to experience expansion and spontaneity

Be willing to undertake any duties

Encourage others

God's love is voluntary

To give heart and soul

Angels give unconditionally

Being enthusiastic makes work a lot easier

Enthusiasm should be contagious

## LOVE is sensational

*Illumination*

LOVE always lights the way

# ～ 29 ～
## *Illumination*

An energy around the throne of God

Seek Divine wisdom and guidance

Lighting the pathway

Illumination is to walk hand in hand with Angels

Illumination brings light into the darkness of the minds of everyone

Bring light upon this earth

Word of prayer

Inspiration and creativity

Allow your light to shine for all to see

LOVE always lights the way

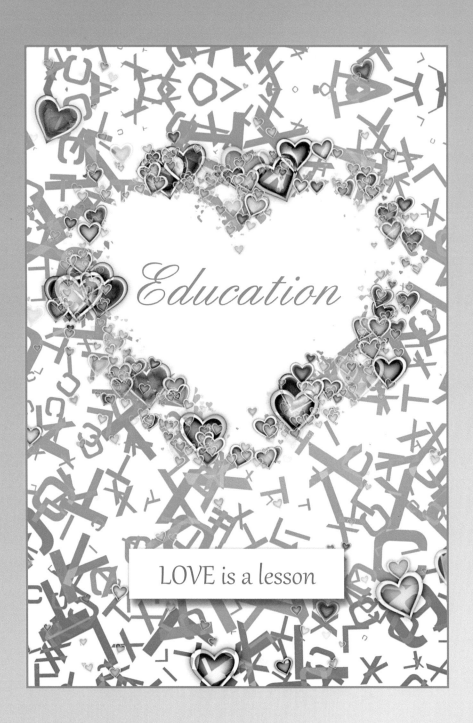

# Education

## LOVE is a lesson

# ❦ 30 ❧
# *Education*

Be a willing scholar

Education broadens mind and horizons

Teach others

We each teach one another

Educate the children

Teach by example

Learn new skills

Be ready to pass on your gifts

God teaches us the way

## LOVE is a lesson

# Willingness

## LOVE is better when free

# ❧ 31 ❧
## *Willingness*

Giving Love

Be of service to all

Angels willingly come to help when called

Give from the heart unconditionally

God willingly listens to your prayers

Better to volunteer

Always be ready and willing to listen

Be willing to learn

Help will arrive when it is needed

## LOVE is better when free

# Flexibility

LOVE goes with the flow

# ❦ 32 ❧
## *Flexibility*

Do not be rigid

Be like a tree that bends in the wind

Flexibility allows movement

Flexibility is another opportunity to learn

God would like us all to be flexible

If your mind is flexible your body is more supple

There is always another way

Angels are lithe

You can advance so much more

## LOVE goes with the flow

# Self-Worth

LOVE is learning to love yourself

# ❧ 33 ☙
## *Self-Worth*

Believe in yourself

Begin to Love yourself

Build on self-esteem

Respect yourself

Learn to say 'no'

God believes in you

Angels will always love you

Take pride in yourself

Don't give yourself a hard time or put yourself down

## LOVE is learning to love yourself

# Meditation

### LOVE gets better with practice

# ❧ 34 ❧
# *Meditation*

Sit still-enter into silence

Still the mind; empty it so it can be filled

Meditation brings answers to your questions

God is waiting to reply

Explore your full potential

Meet with Angels

Attunements

Tap into resources and knowledge

Develop your gifts

## LOVE gets better with practice

# Blessings

LOVE is to cherish

# ❧ 35 ❧
# *Blessings*

Count your blessings one by one

Blessings are gifts from God

Blessings are messages from Angels

Take nothing for granted

Bless your daily bread

Bless all you have within your life

Sight, sound, mobility, speech and freedom are all blessings

Bless all you meet upon your pathway

Blessings may come in disguise

## LOVE is to cherish

# Commitment

LOVE is not a duty - it comes naturally

# ❧ 36 ☙
# *Commitment*

Never break a promise

Don't commit if you're going to quit

God is devoted to duty

Angels teach us love and devotion

Weigh up all pros and cons

It's not what you give up, it's what you can gain

Don't bend the rules

Learn to be of service to all

Have the dedication to perform a duty

## LOVE is not a duty - it comes naturally

# Courage

LOVE won't let you down

# ❧ 37 ☙
## Courage

You can face all adversity

Make a stand and be counted

Unite within the power of God

Within all the hustle and bustle, go thy way placidly

Angels will form a shield for you

Walk your talk

Have the determination to overcome any obstacles or barriers

Be brave enough to face any challenge life will offer you

Walk tall, walk straight with pride and dignity

## LOVE won't let you down

# Justice

LOVE outweighs all

# ❧ 38 ❧
## *Justice*

Love will solve all issues and problems

Deliver unto the hands of God and the Angels

The outcome will be favourable

If indecisive weigh it all up

Fairness in all things

Seek professional guidance

Heed Universal Law

Do unto others as you would have others do unto you

To thine own self be true

## LOVE outweighs all

# Humour

## LOVE ENJOYS LAUGHTER

# ❦ 39 ❧
## *Humour*

Laughter is a great healer

Laugh and the whole world joins in

Release tension, negativity and disharmony

Laugh daily

God has a wonderful sense of humour

Smile at all you meet and greet

Laughter draws Angels nearer

Children adore laughter to thrive

Spread happiness wherever you go

LOVE enjoys laughter

# Harmony

LOVE is coming together

# ⋆§ 40 §⋆
## *Harmony*

Everything in tune

Blending mind, body and spirit

Within God's hand there is harmony

Balance within

Become one with nature

Play all the right notes

Angelic voices are melodious

Harmony is walking hand in hand

Being side by side, step by step

LOVE is coming together

# Beauty

LOVE is always beautiful

# ❧ 41 ❧
# *Beauty*

True picture of God

Always look within the eyes of beauty

Look for beauty within the character

Beauty is in the eyes of the beholder

Beauty is like a flower

Work with beauty all around you

May your mind be filled with beauty

May the beauty within radiate far and wide

Beauty is the heart of an Angel

LOVE is always beautiful

# Comfort

LOVE is a refreshing change

# ❦ 42 ❧
## *Comfort*

Be at one with self and all

Offer condolences

God's love will always bring comfort

Angelic relief

Look on the brighter side

Be uplifted and joyful

Refresh the body, soul and mind

Comfort brings hope and salvation

Offer comfort to all those who are spiritually lost

## LOVE is a refreshing change

# Inspiration

LOVE is a gift to share

# ❧ 43 ❧
## *Inspiration*

All gifts are inspired

Use inspiration to manifest here on earth

Inspiration is an idea, a thought; guidance

Inspiration – a gift from God

Inspiration gives birth to something new

Inspiration brings joy and hopefulness

Angelic enthusiasm

The Universe thrives and grows on inspiration

Inspiration brings light

## LOVE is a gift to share

# Faith

LOVE has no doubts

# ❧ 44 ❧
## *Faith*

Trust and believe

In darkest moments faith is tried and tested

God will not let you down

Faith cannot be seen or heard – only experienced

Faith is a support when in the darkness

Believe in miracles

With faith Angels fly higher

All of nature and creatures have faith

What have you to lose?

## LOVE has no doubts

# Gratitude

LOVE's song is thankfulness

# ❧ 45 ☙
# *Gratitude*

Always being grateful creates an opportunity for growth

Appreciate and acknowledge all within your life

Do not take anything for granted

Be truly thankful

Really open your eyes and your heart

Angels serve with gratitude

God shows gratitude by creativity and inspiration

No matter how difficult your journey, accept with gratitude

Your progress will go from strength to strength

## LOVE's song is thankfulness

# Efficiency

LOVE can only get better

# ❧ 46 ❧
## *Efficiency*

Improve all aspects of yourself

Be consistent and persevere

Efficiency does not give up or give in

God shows by example

Practice as much and as often as it takes

Angels always deliver on time

If you are efficient you will see a result from all your effort

To achieve, to accomplish, to succeed; be efficient

Love can be successful

## LOVE can only get better

# *Wisdom*

LOVE teaches us to be compassionate

# ❧ 47 ❧
# *Wisdom*

Wise words, wise actions

Seek a higher knowledge

Wisdom knows no age barrier

Wisdom is more powerful than the sword

God will impart his wisdom to you

Wisdom unravels all mystery

Wisdom is a wise head and a still tongue

Wisdom – Angelic guidance

Powerful – be as wise as King Solomon

LOVE teaches us to be compassionate

# Joy

LOVE brings pleasure

# 48
## *Joy*

Joy brings upliftment

Joy illuminates darkness

Enjoyment, leisure and pleasure

Have happiness in what you undertake

God loves mirth

Angels love to bring joy to all

Hearts uplifted mend quicker

Joy makes footsteps lighter

Look at all things money cannot buy

LOVE brings pleasure

Trust

LOVE is letting go

# ❦ 49 ❧
## *Trust*

Total belief in God

Do not be afraid

Dismiss all fear and anxiety

Angels will not let you fall

Let go, let God

Believe in power of prayer

Trust - like a baby who takes their first faltering steps

Become more in tune with your senses

Listen to your inner voice

LOVE is letting go

# Light

LOVE will not weigh you down

# ❧ 50 ❧
## *Light*

An energy which is powerful

Angelic power is light

Expand the light within

May your light brighten up this world

Allow your light to shine, to show others the way

God's light will illuminate your path

Don't trip up – always look to the light

Your journey will be easier when guided by the light

Why be in the darkness when there is light?

## LOVE will not weigh you down

# Peace

LOVE is quietness

# ❧ 51 ☙
## *Peace*

Quietness and stillness

Be at one within and without

Accept Yourself

Walk within the beauty of God

Be still within your mind

Enter Peace and enter Silence

Build your Temple within

Do not hasten through the hustle and bustle

Find gentleness within the heart

## LOVE is quietness

# Clarity

LOVE has vision

# ❦ 52 ❧
## *Clarity*

Look at everything with a clearer mind

Take time out to pause, stop and look around

Dance, sing, play; release fears and negativity

God's vision is all-seeing and knowing

Angels always see a brighter picture

Don't let stubbornness hinder your progress

Everything is always made clear when the time is right

De-clutter – the answer may be right in front of you

Take off the blinkers and you will see a much bigger picture

## LOVE has vision

# Truth

LOVE is the right thing to do

## ❦ 53 ❧
### *Truth*

The knowledge is within your heart

Be true to yourself

God's word

Stand and be counted

Truth will always be victor

Look another straight in the eye

Truth has no twists and turns

Truth does not bend

Angelic honesty

LOVE is the right thing to do

# Purification

LOVE will cleanse heart and soul

# ⌁ 54 ⌁
## *Purification*

Purify all thoughts

Cleanse and release all negativity

God will purify your pathway to expand your consciousness

Do not harbour or bear a grudge

Purify heart and mind

Angelic holiness

Be ready to progress

The way is to move forward

Do, with the purest of intention

LOVE will cleanse heart and soul

# Honesty

LOVE is being open

# ❧ 55 ❧
## *Honesty*

Being open

Frankness with kindness

Being trustworthy

Honesty has nothing to hide

Respect for yourself

God relies on you to be honest

Be honest with others

Gain trust and confidence

We can always trust in the Angels

LOVE is being open

# Bliss

LOVE is all relaxed

# ❧ 56 ❧
## *Bliss*

Angelic caresses

Allow yourself the bliss of total relaxation

Release cares, woes and worries

Allow God's gentleness to wash over you

Answers will come when you learn to tune in

Watch the sunrise, sunset, the bird on its wing

Poetry in motion

Bliss can be water as it laps to the shore and washes over stones

A beautiful rose or flower

LOVE is all relaxed

# Acknowledge

LOVE is easily recognised

# ❧ 57 ☙
## *Acknowledge*

Meet and greet your fellow man

God showers you with blessings

Recognise that help is always available

Acknowledge all the many wonderful gifts around you

We are all united and connected to the whole of the Universe

Each experience is an opportunity for progress and expansion

Power of Angels

Appreciate all within your life

Open your eyes and your heart

LOVE is easily recognised

# Healing

LOVE is to mend

# ❦ 58 ❦
## *Healing*

Divine comfort from God and the Angels

A loving thought can be healing

Release your blockages

Healing can bring relief

Healing prevents dis-ease

An Angel caress

Experience pure bliss

Healing leaves no scars

You can heal – just try

## LOVE is to mend

# Simplicity

LOVE is always pure

# ⛤59⛤
## *Simplicity*

Keep everything plain and simple

Do not clutter

Do not make it complicated

You are a child in God's eyes

Look through the eyes of children

Nature is a wonderful teacher

Purity – an essence of the Angels

When it is simple everyone understands

Simplicity is truth and beauty

LOVE is always pure

# Happiness

LOVE is to be joyful

# ✿ 60 ✿
# *Happiness*

Embrace the feeling of joy

Laughter releases all ills

The worst is over

Smile across your heart

Like sunshine, happiness brings warmth

Angels are rejoicing in happiness

Happiness is a Creation of God – a blessing

Laugh and the whole world will join you

Happiness is music to the ear

LOVE is to be joyful

# Prayer

LOVE always listens

# ❦ 61 ❧
## *Prayer*

Communication with God

Talk over any worries, problems or concerns with God

A request for help

To ask on behalf of others

Send prayers out to the world

Prayers can link any time; day or night

Angels listen

Absent healing

Prayer relieves and releases stress, tension and negativity

## LOVE always listens

# Patience

LOVE is steadfast

# ❧ 62 ❧
## *Patience*

Patience is a virtue you need to master

Nature is a wonderful teacher

God never runs out of patience with you

Patience can teach you many attributes

We yearn for more

Angelic perseverance

Be tolerant with one another

Patience is always well rewarded

Take one day at a time

## LOVE is steadfast

*Acceptance*

LOVE always approves

# ❧ 63 ☙
## *Acceptance*

Learn to believe in yourself

Approve of yourself

God accepts your individuality

Learn to accept the uniqueness in others

Believing in yourself will make your confidence soar

Receive praise graciously

Angelic compliment

Accept what is beyond your power to change

An accepting attitude will help you gain inner Peace

## LOVE always approves